A MIDSUMMER NIGHT'S DREAM: A GUIDE

The Shakespeare Handbooks

Available now:

- Antony & Cleopatra
- As You Like It
- Hamlet
- King Lear
- Macbeth
- A Midsummer Night's Dream
- Romeo & Juliet
- Twelfth Night

Forthcoming titles include:

- The Tempest
- Julius Caesar

The Shakespeare Handbooks are available at bookshops, or direct from the publisher: see back page for details.

A Midsummer Night's Dream

A Guide

by Alistair McCallum

Upstart Crow Publications

First published in 1998 by
Upstart Crow Publications

A CIP catalogue record for this book
is available from the British Library

ISBN 1 899747 09 5

Printed in Great Britain by Redwood Books,
Kennet Way, Trowbridge, Wiltshire BA14 8RN

Upstart Crow Publications is a division of
The Language Studio Ltd
11 St John's Terrace
Lewes, East Sussex, U.K.
BN7 2DL
01273 477626

Setting the scene

Shakespeare wrote *A Midsummer Night's Dream* in or around 1595. He had just turned thirty, and was already developing a formidable reputation as a playwright and poet. He had left his native Stratford-on-Avon for London some five years before, and was by now a member of the most prestigious and successful acting company in the capital, his plays receiving acclaim both at the public playhouses and at the court of Queen Elizabeth.

A severe outbreak of the plague, which had resulted in the closure of the London theatres for two years, was now over; the theatres were back in business, and Shakespeare, who had meanwhile been devoting his time to poetry, returned to playwriting. The results were spectacular. *Romeo and Juliet*, his tragedy of the two young lovers, caused a sensation; and *A Midsummer Night's Dream*, which followed soon afterwards, was another resounding success.

Although the play was undoubtedly written for the public stage, it is likely that the first performance of *A Midsummer Night's Dream* was at a wedding-party attended by the Queen. Ten years later, the same play was to be performed at the court of her successor, King James, another great admirer of Shakespeare. However, Shakespeare's appeal was never limited to courtly circles; his great strength as a dramatist was his enduring popularity with the public. *A Midsummer Night's Dream*, like so much of his work, possesses a richness, complexity and resonance that have proved irresistible to audiences throughout the years:

"It is some measure of the play's strength that it is almost infallibly entertaining under any circumstances... It is not simply by a happy accident that A Midsummer Night's Dream *has retained for four centuries its power to entertain. Rather it is because this is a highly articulated structure, the product of a genius working with total mastery of his poetic and theatrical craft."*

Stanley Wells, Introduction to *A Midsummer Night's Dream*, 1967

War gives way to love

Theseus, Duke of Athens, has returned home victorious from the wars.

Among the Duke's conquests is the distant eastern land of Scythia, home of the Amazon warrior women. He has captured the Amazon Queen, Hippolyta, and brought her back to Athens: the two of them have fallen in love, and are soon to be married.

Curtain up

A disobedient daughter

Duke Theseus is impatient. His marriage to Hippolyta will take place in four days' time, when the new crescent moon appears in the heavens: and the days seem to be dragging by with unbearable sluggishness. Hippolyta reassures him that the time will soon pass:

> *Hippolyta:* Four days will quickly steep themselves* in night;
> Four nights will quickly dream away the time;
> And then the moon, like to a silver bow
> New bent in heaven, shall behold the night
> Of our solemnities.**
>
> ** sink, immerse themselves*
> *** celebrations*

Theseus tells Philostrate, his Master of the Revels, to prepare festivities throughout Athens in celebration of his forthcoming marriage. He is determined that the wedding, in contrast to the violent struggle that preceded it, will be a happy and memorable occasion:

> *Theseus:* Hippolyta, I woo'd thee with my sword,
> And won thy love doing thee injuries;
> But I will wed thee in another key,
> With pomp, with triumph, and with revelling.

As Philostrate leaves, Egeus, an Athenian courtier, comes before the Duke, accompanied by his daughter Hermia. Following them are two young men, Demetrius and Lysander.

Egeus has come to ask for the Duke's help. He has decided, he explains, that his daughter is to marry Demetrius: but, to his exasperation, she has fallen in love with Lysander, and now refuses absolutely to go along with her father's wishes. Egeus accuses Lysander of tricking Hermia into loving him in a multitude of subtle, deceitful ways:

Egeus: Thou, thou, Lysander, thou hast given her rhymes,
            And interchang'd love-tokens with my child:
            Thou hast by moonlight at her window sung
            With faining* voice verses of feigning love,
            And stol'n the impression of her fantasy**
            With bracelets of thy hair, rings, gauds, conceits,
            Knacks, trifles, nosegays...

* soft, quiet
** captured her imagination

Infuriated at his daughter's disobedience, Egeus delivers a public ultimatum. If she continues to reject Demetrius, he will assert his right as a father, as enshrined in Athenian law:

Egeus: ... Be it so she will not here, before your Grace,
            Consent to marry with Demetrius,
            I beg the ancient privilege of Athens:
            As she is mine, I may dispose of her;
            Which shall be either to this gentleman,
            Or to her death...

Gently but firmly, Theseus tells Hermia that she should obey her father, regardless of her feelings for Lysander. Hermia asks him what the judgement of the law would be if she should refuse to marry Demetrius. The Duke confirms that, as her father said, she may be put to death if she chooses to marry Lysander. Her only escape from the death penalty, he explains, would be to spend the rest of her life in a nunnery, utterly renouncing the company of men for ever.

Although he is full of admiration for those who live in the celibacy and isolation of a nunnery, Theseus warns Hermia that this would not be an easy path to follow, especially at her young age:

> *Theseus:*   ... examine well your blood,
> Whether, if you yield not to your father's choice,
> You can endure the livery* of a nun,
> For aye** to be in shady cloister mew'd,***
> To live a barren sister all your life,
> Chanting faint hymns to the cold fruitless moon.
>
> ** clothing, habit*
> *** for ever*
> **** cooped up*

Hermia immediately declares that she will choose life in a nunnery rather than marry a man she does not love. The Duke tells her to wait before making up her mind: when the time comes for his own wedding to Hippolyta, he will ask Hermia for her final decision.

Demetrius urges Hermia to obey her father, and calls on Lysander to give up his claim to Hermia's love. Lysander responds heatedly. He is as good a man as Demetrius, he declares; besides, Hermia loves him, not Demetrius.

Moreover, Lysander reveals, Demetrius already has an admirer: her name is Helena, and Demetrius claimed to be in love with her before he met Hermia. Helena, though rejected, is still devoted to Demetrius. Lysander accuses his rival of inconstancy, a charge that Demetrius is unable to deny.

The lovers remain defiant

With a final warning to Hermia that there will be serious consequences if she disregards her father's decision, Theseus leaves. Hippolyta is dismayed: but the law must be obeyed, insists the Duke, come what may. He too is unhappy with the situation, and asks Demetrius and Egeus to go with him so that they can discuss the matter in private.

The two lovers are left alone to contemplate their plight. Lysander tries to comfort Hermia. Lovers have always faced obstacles, he assures her:

Lysander: ... For aught* that I could ever read,
             Could ever hear by tale or history,
             The course of true love never did run smooth...

   * *from anything*

Even when love has not been thwarted by family hostilities, one legend after another shows how it has always proved precarious and brief:

Lysander: ... if there were a sympathy in choice,*
War, death, or sickness did lay siege to it,
Making it momentary as a sound,
Swift as a shadow, short as any dream,
Brief as the lightning in the collied** night,
That, in a spleen, unfolds*** both heaven and earth,
And, ere a man hath power to say 'Behold!',
The jaws of darkness do devour it up:
So quick bright things come to confusion.

even if no-one was against the match
**coal-black*
***reveals, in a fit of passion*

> *"There is no play of Shakespeare's that demands such sustained delicacy of treatment. Story and characters both are kept - are constantly being reined - within the bounds of gentleness. The verse has the virtues of chamber music. It is never robustly declamatory; it asks constantly for a quiet clarity of utterance... it has neither sharp turns of phrase, nor sudden checking of pace, nor one twisted or tortured thought. It flows on like a river in sunlight."*
>
> Harley Granville-Barker, Preface to *The Players' Shakespeare* edition, 1924

If love has always been so fraught with problems, reflects Hermia, the two of them must be prepared to face hardship. Lysander agrees; but something occurs to him that might allow them to marry whilst escaping the retribution demanded by Hermia's father.

About twenty miles from Athens lives Lysander's aunt, a wealthy, childless widow who treats the young man like a son. If he and Hermia can reach her house, explains Lysander, they will be beyond the power of the Athenian law, and the two of them can marry in safety. He asks Hermia to slip away from her father's house tomorrow night, in secrecy, and meet him in the wood just outside Athens. It is a place they both know; they once met there, early one May morning, in a ceremony celebrating the arrival of summer. From the wood they can make their way to the widow's house, where they will be married.

Hermia agrees to the plan without hesitation, and gives Lysander her word that she will join him tomorrow night. Her promise is given solemnly, but she cannot resist teasing Lysander about the fickleness of men:

Hermia: ... I swear to thee by Cupid's strongest bow,
              By his best arrow with the golden head,
              By the simplicity* of Venus' doves...
              By all the vows that ever men have broke
              (In number more than ever women spoke),
              In that same place thou hast appointed me,
              Tomorrow truly will I meet with thee.

        harmlessness, gentleness

Helena learns a secret

Helena now joins the two lovers. She is hopelessly in love with Demetrius, and desperately wishes that he loved her instead of Hermia. She asks her friend how she has managed to enchant Demetrius, but Hermia admits that she is baffled. She has done everything she can to persuade Demetrius that his love is unwanted, but without success:

Helena: O, teach me how you look, and with what art
              You sway* the motion of Demetrius' heart.
Hermia: I frown upon him; yet he loves me still.
Helena: O that your frowns would teach my smiles such skill!
Hermia: I give him curses; yet he gives me love.
Helena: O that my prayers could such affection move!
Hermia: The more I hate, the more he follows me.
Helena: The more I love, the more he hateth me.
Hermia: His folly, Helena, is no fault of mine.
Helena: None but your beauty; would that fault were mine!

     * *govern, control*

However, Hermia has some comforting news for Helena. She explains that she and Lysander plan to elope tomorrow, under cover of darkness. Demetrius will never see her again; perhaps his affection for Helena will be rekindled.

Hermia, who has been Helena's friend since childhood, now bids her a fond farewell, and leaves to prepare for her escape. Lysander leaves too, with a final wish that Helena's love for Demetrius will eventually be returned.

Left on her own, Helena reflects on the unfairness and illogicality of love. Everyone else believes that she is as beautiful as Hermia, but Demetrius seems to be unaware of her beauty.

It is with good reason that Cupid is always shown blindfolded in pictures, Helena realises:

Helena: Love looks not with the eyes, but with the mind,
             And therefore is wing'd Cupid painted blind...

Demetrius used to love her, and even though he has proved himself inconstant Helena cannot stop loving him. She decides, on a sudden impulse, to tell Demetrius about the elopement. In all probability he will set off at once in pursuit of Hermia; but at least he will be grateful to Helena for the revelation, and his gratitude will give her something to treasure.

Love looks not with the eyes, but with the mind...

One of the many themes woven into the fabric of *A Midsummer Night's Dream* is sight: the eyes are mentioned more often in this play than in any other. The emphasis, however, is on the deceptiveness of appearances and the constant possibility of misunderstanding or misinterpreting what we see. This preoccupation has given the play a particular significance for our own age:

"... it was not until the twentieth century that scholars began to comprehend the philosophical depth and dramatic complexity of Shakespeare's creation. What was once considered a light, insubstantial play or fairy tale is now regarded as one of Shakespeare's most satisfying works, and a keen dramatic investigation into concerns he was to treat more seriously in his later comedies and tragedies: the nature of love, the influence of the spiritual world on the mortal, the conflict between appearance and reality... Shakespeare was nearing the height of his powers as a comic playwright."

Mark W. Scott, *Shakespearean Criticism*, 1986

An amateur dramatic society assembles

A group of workmen has gathered to prepare for a play which they intend to perform in honour of Duke Theseus' wedding. Quince, a carpenter, is in charge, and he starts by checking that everyone is present. However, he is immediately interrupted by Nick Bottom, a weaver, who cannot resist advising Quince on the running of the meeting:

Bottom: First, good Peter Quince, say what the play treats on; then read the names of the actors; and so grow to a point.

Quince: Marry, our play is 'The most Lamentable Comedy, and most Cruel Death of Pyramus and Thisbe'.

Bottom: A very good piece of work, I assure you, and a merry. Now, good Peter Quince, call forth your actors...

Quince proceeds to call out the names of the participants. Bottom is first on the list. Confirming that he is present, he asks what role he is to play; Quince replies that he has the part of Pyramus, a lover whose passion drives him to a noble, tragic suicide. Bottom immediately becomes excited at the prospect of moving the audience to tears, although his speciality, he explains, is in playing powerful, blustering roles like Hercules. He gives a brief, noisy demonstration, then assures the others that he will play the part of a lover more tenderly. Finally, Quince is allowed to continue with his roll call.

Flute, the bellows-mender, is told that he is to play Thisbe, Pyramus's beloved. Flute is disappointed; he would rather not play the part of a woman, as he is convinced that his meagre beard is starting to grow. The irrepressible Bottom volunteers to play Thisbe as well as Pyramus, and gives another impromptu demonstration of his acting prowess; but Quince rules against him.

All the workmen in the amateur company have names fitting to their trades. Quince is probably named after the 'quoins' or wooden wedges that he uses as a carpenter. A 'bottom' is the core around which the weaver's yarn is wound. Flute as a bellows-mender would repair the pipes of church organs, while a tinker would mend the 'snout' or spout of a kettle. A joiner's work should be 'snug' or tight-fitting.

The name of Robin Starveling reflects the fact that tailors were traditionally poor and undernourished. This part, incidentally, was undoubtedly written for John Sincler, the 'thin man' of Shakespeare's acting company. Other roles written with the emaciated Sincler in mind crop up in many of Shakespeare's plays, including *Romeo and Juliet* and *The Comedy of Errors*.

Quince now announces the casting of the remaining parts. The emaciated Robin Starveling, a tailor, will play Thisbe's mother: Tom Snout the tinker will be Pyramus's father: and Quince himself will play Thisbe's father. The final member of the cast is Snug, the joiner, who will play the part of a lion.

Snug is apprehensive; he admits to being a slow learner, and requests a copy of his part as soon as possible so that he has time to memorise it. Quince reassures him that no learning is involved; all he needs to do is give the occasional roar. Nick Bottom barges in again, volunteering to play the lion. Once again Quince rules against him; his roaring would terrify Theseus' bride and the other ladies. Bottom promises to be considerate:

Bottom: ... I will aggravate my voice so, that I will roar you as gently as any sucking dove; I will roar you and* 'twere any nightingale.

        * *as if*

Bottom must play Pyramus, insists Quince: the role is a heroic, gallant one, and demands an actor of Bottom's stature. Bottom is satisfied, but immediately becomes engrossed in another topic: what should be the colour of Pyramus's beard? As a weaver he is familiar with many dyes, but his choice of possible colours - gold, orange, purple or yellow - is questionable.

Quince now hands out the various parts for the actors to study, asking them all to learn their lines by tomorrow night. In order to keep the whole project secret, he has decided that they will rehearse at night, by moonlight, in a wood just outside Athens.

There was a wide range of theatrical activity in Shakespeare's day. Although there were relatively few professional companies like Shakespeare's own, there were many semi-professional and amateur groups who put on shows at weddings, parties and fairs, and there were plenty of tavern comedians, clowns, fools, dancers and acrobats. While plays and shows were popular at the royal Court and at many great houses, there was strong resistance from Puritans who had an increasingly powerful influence in the Church and in local government. One of the most vociferous opponents was an ex-playwright who underwent a radical change of heart in his twenties and became a Puritan clergyman:

"The argument of tragedies is wrath, cruelty, incest, injury, murder... the ground-work of comedies is love, cozenage,* flattery, bawdry, sly conveyance of whoredom... what schooling is this? Sometime you shall see nothing but the adventures of an amorous knight, passing from country to country for the love of his lady, encountering many a terrible monster made of brown paper... What learn you by that? When the soul of your plays is either mere trifles, or Italian bawdry, or wooing of gentlewomen, what are ye taught?"

* trickery

Stephen Gosson, *Playes Confuted in Five Actions*, 1582

The spirit world is revealed

The Athenian wood is home to a host of fairies and spirits, invisible to humans. Two such beings now meet. One is an attendant of the Fairy Queen, Titania, and the other serves Oberon, King of the fairy world. As Titania's follower says, the obstacles of the human world are no barrier to the spirits as they go about their business:

> *Fairy:* Over hill, over dale,
>   Thorough* bush, thorough briar,
>   Over park,** over pale,***
>   Thorough flood, thorough fire,
>   I do wander everywhere...
>
> ** through*
> *** enclosed hunting land*
> **** ground surrounded by fences*

Oberon's servant reveals that his master and Titania have fallen out. The Queen has stolen a little boy from the mortal world: and Oberon wants the changeling, the son of an Indian King, as one of his followers. Titania, however, is keeping the boy for herself, pampering him and bedecking him with flowers. The changeling is the subject of continual argument between the Fairy King and Queen:

> *Puck:*   ... now they never meet in grove or green,
>   By fountain clear, or spangled starlight sheen,*
>   But they do square;** that all their elves for fear
>   Creep into acorn-cups, and hide them there.
>
> ** gleaming, shining*
> *** quarrel, confront one another*

Titania's fairy suddenly recognises Oberon's attendant as Robin Goodfellow, the notorious spirit also known as Puck, renowned for his mischievous interference in human affairs:

Fairy: Are you not he
That frights the maidens of the villagery,
Skim milk, and sometimes labour in the quern,
And bootless make the breathless housewife churn,*
And sometime make the drink to bear no barm,**
Mislead night-wanderers, laughing at their harm?

* *steal the cream from milk, so that the housewife becomes exhausted in her fruitless effort to make butter in the churn*
** *take the froth from the ale, make it flat*

Puck proudly confirms that the fairy is right. He gleefully describes some of the tricks he plays to amuse his master Oberon, tricks which cause the everyday mishaps that mortals find so inexplicable:

Puck: ... sometime lurk I in a gossip's bowl
In very likeness of a roasted crab,*
And when she drinks, against her lips I bob,
And on her wither'd dewlap** pour the ale.

* *roasted crab apple, sometimes put in spiced ale to add flavour*
** *sagging chin*

Puck is interrupted by the entrance of his master Oberon: and at the same time, coming from the opposite direction, Titania approaches.

Belief in mischievous fairies and spirits was fairly widespread in Shakespeare's day, particularly in rural areas. Robin Goodfellow - probably so named to avoid giving offence to the elusive creature - was believed by the superstitious to carry out malicious pranks if not treated kindly. If a bowl of milk and bread was left out for him at night, on the other hand, he would cause no trouble, and might even perform unaccountable good turns around the house.

"The creature variously called puck, pouka, pixie, bugbear and hobgoblin, as well as the other fairies, was dangerous, and an Elizabethan audience could not contemplate him or his associates as representatives of the unknown without some apprehension."

David Young, *Something of Great Constancy*, 1966

Discord among the fairies

As Puck had predicted, Oberon and Titania clash at once. The Fairy Queen threatens to make a dramatic exit as soon as she sets eyes on the King:

> *Oberon:* Ill met by moonlight, proud Titania.
> *Titania:* What, jealous Oberon? Fairies, skip hence;
> I have forsworn* his bed and company.
>
> * *sworn to avoid*

Oberon orders Titania to stay: but he has lost his right to give her orders, she replies, by his relentless pursuit of women of the mortal world. She names Hippolyta, shortly to be married, as one of his recent loves. Oberon retorts that he is well aware of Titania's own attempts to entice the mortal Theseus.

Titania in turn accuses Oberon of jealousy and bad temper. As a result of his angry squabbling, she says, their fairy rituals have been disturbed, with dire consequences for the natural world:

Titania: ... the winds, piping to us in vain,*
                 As in revenge have suck'd up from the sea
                 Contagious fogs; which, falling in the land,
                 Hath every pelting river made so proud
                 That they have overborne their continents.**
                 The ox hath therefore stretch'd his yoke in vain,
                 The ploughman lost*** his sweat, and the green corn
                 Hath rotted ere his youth attain'd a beard...

                 * finding that we fairies have ignored their tune
                 ** paltry little rivers have become so full that they have
                       burst their banks
                 *** wasted

To spectators at the first performances of *A Midsummer Night's Dream*, Titania's description of the weather must have seemed all too appropriate. The summers of 1594 and 1595 were exceptionally cold and wet, with frosts and floods leading to poor harvests and severe shortages of corn. There was widespread discontent at the practices of forestalling - buying corn direct from farmers - and hoarding, both of which made the shortages worse, leading to exorbitantly high prices on the open market. Public anger was intensified by the fact that much of the stored corn was not even used for the baking of bread; a greater profit was to be made from selling the malted grain to brewers.

Despite the public outcry, many of those who could afford to do so built up considerable stockpiles of corn over the following years. In the town of Stratford-on-Avon in 1598, a survey revealed that seventy-five householders possessed stores of grain on their premises. One of the more substantial stores - about eighty bushels - belonged to a prosperous citizen who had just bought the second largest house in the town, Mr William Shakespeare.

It is unseasonably wet and cold in the human world, and disease is rife: and the root cause of all this, claims Titania, is their quarrel over the changeling boy. Oberon maintains that the solution is simply for Titania to hand the boy over to him as he has demanded.

Titania now explains why the human boy is so precious to her. The child's mother had been a devotee of hers, and Titania, descending to the mortal world, had befriended her. During the woman's pregnancy, the two of them had spent long hours together, enjoying one another's company:

Titania: ... in the spiced Indian air, by night,
Full often hath she gossip'd by my side;
And sat with me on Neptune's yellow sands,*
Marking th'embarked traders on the flood:**
When we have laugh'd to see the sails conceive
And grow big-bellied with the wanton wind...

the shore, realm of the sea-god Neptune
** *watching the merchant ships as they set out to sea*

The woman had died in childbirth: and Titania, out of her love for the boy's mother, decided to take the child into the spirit world and look after him.

Oberon remains adamant: he will gladly end their quarrel, but only if Titania surrenders the changeling boy to him. She refuses, and sweeps out with her entourage of fairies.

A magical flower

Oberon is determined to take revenge on Titania for her stubbornness. Calling for his assistant Puck, he asks him to remember a time when they heard a mermaid singing so beautifully that the rough sea suddenly grew calm, and stars fell from the skies. At that time, he reveals, he saw Cupid himself in flight, armed with his bow, invisible to all but Oberon. He describes how Cupid shot a golden arrow at an unsuspecting maiden, Queen of a western land:

Oberon: ... a certain aim he took
At a fair vestal,* throned by the west,
And loos'd his love-shaft smartly from his bow
As** it should pierce a hundred thousand hearts.

* *woman sworn to a life of celibacy*
** *as if*

... a fair vestal, throned by the west...

This is undoubtedly a veiled compliment to Queen Elizabeth, who prided herself on her status as the Virgin Queen and remained resolutely unmarried throughout her life, often claiming that she was 'wedded to her people'.

One of the Queen's goddaughters was married in 1595, and another in 1596; it is highly likely that *A Midsummer Night's Dream* was performed at the wedding-party following one of these marriages. In either case, the Queen herself - a great admirer of Shakespeare - would probably have been in the audience. Many scholars believe that Shakespeare wrote this play with the planned wedding festivities in mind, and the unusually large number of parts for children supports this theory. It is tempting to imagine the excitement and anxiety behind the scenes as the young extras, the wedding over, were marshalled into their dressing-room, helped on with their fairy costumes and ushered on stage to play their part in the big occasion.

But the arrow missed its target, leaving the virgin Queen untroubled by thoughts of love. It landed instead on the ground, where it struck a little wild pansy, changing its colour for ever:

> Oberon: Yet mark'd I where the bolt of Cupid fell:
> It fell upon a little western flower,
> Before milk-white, now purple with love's wound:
> And maidens call it 'love-in-idleness'.

Oberon instructs Puck to fetch this flower. The impact of Cupid's arrow has given it a magical property: if juice from the flower is dropped into the eyes of a sleeping man or woman, they will instantly fall in love, on waking, with the first living creature they see.

As Puck races off to find the flower, Oberon reveals that he plans to drop its juice in Titania's eyes as she sleeps in the wood. On waking, she will fall madly in love with whichever wild creature she first sets eyes on, whether it be a lion, wolf, bear or monkey. He knows of another herb that will act as an antidote to the love-juice; but he will not use it until the changeling boy is his.

Two mortals arrive in the wood

Oberon suddenly becomes aware of two humans who have wandered into the moonlit wood. Making himself invisible, he decides to stay and listen to their conversation.

The first visitor to the wood is Demetrius, who has come in search of Hermia; Helena has told him of her friend's secret elopement and planned marriage to Lysander. In hot pursuit of Demetrius is Helena herself, desperate to be near her beloved; Demetrius, equally desperate, is trying to rid himself of her company. He tries using threats, insults, and appeals to her common sense, but without success; she is determined to be with him at all costs. Even when he runs off, threatening violence if she should follow, Helena does not give up:

> *Helena:* I'll follow thee, and make a heaven of hell,
> To die upon the hand I love so well.

Oberon is moved by Helena's plight. As the two humans leave, he decides to turn the tables on the young man by making him even more desperate for her company than she is for his.

Puck now returns with the magical flower, and hands it to his master. Oberon knows the secret place where Titania sometimes rests:

> *Oberon:* I know a bank where the wild thyme blows,
> Where oxlips and the nodding violet grows,
> Quite over-canopied with luscious woodbine,
> With sweet musk-roses, and with eglantine.
> There sleeps Titania sometime of the night,
> Lull'd in these flowers with dances and delight...

Oberon sets off to drop the love-juice in Titania's eyes. Before leaving, he gives some of the juice from the flower to Puck, instructing him to place it in the eyes of the young Athenian who is so cold-hearted towards his admirer. He orders Puck to do it while the Athenian girl is nearby, so that the youth will instantly be besotted with the girl to whom he had previously been so cruel.

A spell is cast on Titania II, ii

Titania has come to the spot in the wood where she habitually slumbers. She sends her fairies off to attend to their duties:

> *Titania:*   ... Some to kill cankers* in the musk-rose buds;
> Some war with reremice** for their leathern wings,
> To make my small elves coats; and some keep back
> The clamorous owl, that nightly hoots and wonders
> At our quaint*** spirits.
>
> ** grubs, caterpillars*
> *** bats*
> **** dainty, fine*

The fairies sing, warning snakes, spiders, beetles and other creeping animals to keep away from the Queen. Lulled by the music, Titania drifts off to sleep, and the fairies leave.

Oberon now steals in and quickly drops the juice from the magical flower into Titania's eyes. Urging the sleeping Queen to wake when some ugly, loathsome creature is nearby, he makes a hasty exit.

25

A case of mistaken identity

Lysander and Hermia have met up in the wood, as planned, ready to make their way to the house outside Athens where they intend to marry. However, their journey through the wood has left them exhausted; and to make matters worse, Lysander admits that he has lost the way. They decide to sleep in the wood and continue their journey after daybreak.

Hermia stretches out on a grassy bank. Lysander is about to lie next to her, but she insists that he must sleep at a respectable distance from her. She ignores Lysander's protestations, and the two of them, lying well apart, bid each other a fond goodnight and settle down to sleep.

Puck enters, complaining that he can see no trace of the couple that his master has ordered him to find. To his delight, he now comes across the sleeping mortals. The man is in Athenian dress, as Oberon had mentioned, and the woman is lying some way off.

This is clearly the couple that Oberon has sent him to find, decides Puck; the man must be the unfeeling, cruel Athenian youth, and the woman the admirer whom he has rejected so callously. Puck pours the love-potion into the man's eyes, confident that the youth will wake up infatuated with the woman he had previously scorned. He then sets off to tell Oberon of his success.

A Midsummer Night's Dream embodies many of the innumerable folk tales, legends and beliefs associated with May and midsummer in Shakespeare's day. Many believed that it was the season when madness and magic were prevalent; and dreams at this time of year were taken seriously, as they could predict who one's future partner would be.

In the lovers' flight into the woods, there is a hint of the ancient tradition of a night-time or early morning excursion into the countryside to celebrate the arrival of summer. Such festivals, with their clearly pagan roots, were viewed with disapproval by the Puritans of Shakespeare's time:

"Against* May, Whitsunday, or some other time of the year, every parish, town and village assemble themselves together, both men, women and children, old and young... they go some to the woods and groves, some to the hills and mountains, where they spend all the night in pleasant pastimes; and in the morning they return, bringing with them birch boughs and branches of trees... But their chiefest jewel they bring from thence is their May-pole, which they bring home with great veneration... this May-pole is covered all over with flowers and herbs, bound round about with strings from the top to the bottom, and sometimes painted with variable colours, with two or three hundred men, women and children following it with great devotion. Then they fall to banquet and feast, to leap and dance about it, as the heathen people did at the dedication of their idols..."

* in preparation for

Philip Stubbes, *The Anatomie of Abuses*, 1583

Lysander discovers a new love

Demetrius and Helena now approach. Demetrius is still trying to escape from Helena, who doggedly refuses to leave him. By now, though, she is utterly exhausted by her hopeless pursuit. Demetrius runs off, and Helena stops for a moment to regain her breath. She reflects again on Hermia's good fortune in being admired by Demetrius, unaware that her friend is lying, asleep, only yards away:

> *Helena:* Happy is Hermia, wheresoe'er she lies,
> For she hath blessed and attractive eyes.
> How came her eyes so bright? Not with salt tears;
> If so, my eyes are oftener wash'd than hers.

Suddenly, Helena notices Lysander on the ground. She is terrified that he may be dead, and frantically tries to wake him. She is taken aback by the intensity of his response:

> *Helena:* Lysander, if you live, good sir, awake!
> *Lysander:* [*Waking.*] And run through fire I will for thy sweet sake!

Lysander immediately starts to praise Helena's beauty and sweetness. Remembering that she loves Demetrius, he threatens to kill his rival as soon as he finds him. Helena misunderstands his motive, believing that he is angry at Demetrius for loving Hermia. But Lysander can hardly bear to hear Hermia's name mentioned. He now knows, with absolute certainty, that Helena, not Hermia, is the love of his life.

Lysander insists, moreover, that his new-found passion is not mere infatuation, but the product of his own mature powers of reasoning:

Helena: ... Hermia still loves you; then be content.
Lysander: Content with Hermia? No. I do repent
The tedious minutes I with her have spent.
Not Hermia, but Helena I love:
Who will not change a raven for a dove?
The will of man is by his reason sway'd,*
And reason says you are the worthier maid.

* governed, controlled

Helena is indignant. There can only be one explanation for Lysander's outburst; he is enjoying a joke at her expense, pretending to idolise her to show up her own lack of success with Demetrius. Exasperated, she runs off into the wood, followed devotedly by Lysander.

Hermia awakens with a start, and calls for Lysander. She has been having a terrible nightmare, dreaming that a serpent was eating her heart while her beloved looked on and smiled. The terror of the dream is redoubled when she realises that Lysander has gone. Fearful but determined, she sets off into the wood to find him.

Meanwhile, in her flowery hideaway nearby, Titania, unaware of the drama unfolding around her, sleeps peacefully on.

Bottom is transformed

Peter Quince's company of amateur actors arrives in the wood for their secret rehearsal, and Quince chooses a suitable spot to run through the play.

Before the rehearsal starts, Bottom the weaver, who has been studying the script, has a few proposals for improving the play. First, there is the question of the suicide of the hero, Pyramus. Bottom fears that the lover's death by his own sword will be too much for the ladies. There is general agreement; and the timorous Robin Starveling, the tailor, suggests that they should omit the suicide entirely. Bottom, as ever, has a better plan, one which involves the complete dismantling of dramatic illusion:

> *Bottom:*   ... I have a device* to make all well. Write me a prologue, and let the prologue seem to say we will do no harm with our swords, and that Pyramus is not killed indeed; and for the more better assurance, tell them that I, Pyramus, am not Pyramus, but Bottom the weaver. This will put them out of fear.
>
> * *scheme*

The same idea should apply, they all agree, to the part of the lion. To avoid frightening the ladies in the audience, the actor must ensure that his face is visible through a gap in the lion's costume, and he must address the ladies directly, assuring them that he is not a real lion, but Snug the joiner in disguise.

A couple of problems of staging remain. First, there is the question of providing the moonlight that is to illuminate the meeting of Pyramus and Thisbe:

Quince: ... there is two hard things: that is, to bring the moonlight into a chamber; for you know, Pyramus and Thisbe meet by moonlight.

Snout: Doth the moon shine that night we play our play?

Bottom: ... a calendar! Look in the almanac; find out moonshine...

A quick check in Quince's almanac confirms that the moon will be shining on the night of the play; they can open a window in the Duke's palace, suggests Bottom, to let in the moonlight. However, Quince prefers a more foolproof solution, and decides that an actor carrying a lantern will play the part of Moonshine.

Doth the moon shine that night we play our play?

The moon is mentioned more often in *A Midsummer Night's Dream* than in any other play by Shakespeare. It presides over the worlds of the rulers, the lovers, the workmen and the fairies.

At the time the play was written, the moon was believed to be a smooth, glowing celestial body. However, in the northern Italian city of Padua an ambitious young professor of mathematics was already taking a more scientific interest in the moon; some ten years later, he was to discover that the surface of the moon was in fact covered with valleys, craters and mountains. He also asserted that it glowed not with its own light but with reflected sunlight.

The name of the controversial professor, born in the same year as Shakespeare, was Galileo Galilei. His continuing improvements to the newly-invented telescope led to many further discoveries; however, his rejection of classical astronomical theory, which placed the earth at the centre of the universe, brought him into conflict with the Papal authorities, and he spent the last years of his life under house arrest.

31

The second staging problem is the wall that keeps the two lovers apart. This too can be personified, proposes Bottom, to avoid hauling masonry on and off the stage. An actor adorned with a few lumps of plaster and clay can come on when required, and can use his fingers to indicate the chink in the wall through which the lovers whisper to one another. The various technical difficulties overcome, the rehearsal begins.

At this point, unseen by the actors, Puck enters. He decides to observe the antics of the humans, and, if the fancy takes him, to join in:

> *Puck:* What hempen homespuns* have we swaggering here,
> So near the cradle of the Fairy Queen?
> What, a play toward?** I'll be an auditor;
> An actor too perhaps, if I see cause.
>
> * *roughly clad country bumpkins*
> ** *in preparation*

The run-through commences. Right from the start, Quince is kept busy, prompting his actors and correcting mistakes. After his first speech, Bottom makes his exit, and Puck follows him, intent on mischief. Flute, as Thisbe, now speaks his part. Quince calls out for Pyramus to return: he has missed his cue.

Bottom reappears. He does not realise it, but he has become the victim of Puck's trickery; his head has been replaced with that of an ass. His comrades, almost speechless with fright, cannot find the words to tell poor Bottom what has happened to him:

> *Quince:* O monstrous! O strange! We are haunted! Pray, masters! Fly, masters! Help!... Bless thee, Bottom, bless thee! Thou art translated.

The workmen run off, their panic intensified as Puck pursues them in a series of terrifying guises. Bottom is left alone in the darkness of the wood.

A Midsummer Night's Dream has been a favourite with audiences ever since its first performances. However, one spectator - normally a great admirer of Shakespeare - was unpleasantly surprised. Having earlier decided that his compulsive theatregoing and socialising were taking up too much of his time, he had vowed to give up both going to plays and drinking for four months. His first return to the theatre was a disappointment, although it is only fair to point out that he saw a greatly simplified version of the play, with the emphasis on music and dancing at the expense of the original plot and language.

"Michaelmas day. This day my oaths for drinking of wine and going to plays are out,* and so I do resolve to take a liberty today... to the King's Theatre, where we saw Midsummer nights dreame, *which I have never seen before, nor shall ever again, for it is the most insipid ridiculous play that ever I saw in my life. I saw, I confess, some good dancing and some handsome women, which was all my pleasure."*

* are over, have been fulfilled

Samuel Pepys, diary entry for 29th September 1662

An introduction to the fairy world

Bottom assumes that his friends are playing a prank on him, and are trying to scare him by leaving him on his own in the wood. He refuses to be frightened, and starts singing to show how fearless he is.

Bottom's strident tones awaken Titania, who has been sleeping nearby. The love-potion that Oberon has placed in her eyes takes effect immediately:

> *Titania:* What angel wakes me from my flowery bed?
> ... I pray thee, gentle mortal, sing again:
> Mine ear is much enamour'd of thy note;
> So is mine eye enthralled to thy shape...

Everything about the ass-headed Bottom enchants Titania, and she declares at once that she has fallen in love with him. Bottom responds bashfully and modestly, while the Fairy Queen hangs devotedly on his every word:

> *Bottom:* Methinks, mistress, you should have little reason for that.
> And yet, to say the truth, reason and love keep little
> company together nowadays. The more the pity that
> some honest neighbours will not make them friends...
> *Titania:* Thou art as wise as thou art beautiful.
> *Bottom:* Not so neither...

Bottom mentions that he is anxious to find his way out of the wood. Titania's response to her new love is firm and regal:

> *Titania:* Out of this wood do not desire to go:
> Thou shalt remain here, whether thou wilt or no.
> I am a spirit of no common rate;*
> The summer still doth tend upon my state...**
>
> ** special, high-ranking*
> *** always awaits my command*

The Queen tells Bottom that he will have fairies to attend on him; and eventually, after nights spent on sumptuous beds of flowers, with fairies singing him to sleep, he will become like a spirit himself. She calls for four of her attendants - Peaseblossom, Cobweb, Moth and Mustardseed - and introduces them to her beloved. She instructs them to treat him with the utmost courtesy and devotion:

Titania: ... Feed him with apricocks and dewberries,
                With purple grapes, green figs, and mulberries;
                The honey-bags steal from the humble-bees,
                And for night-tapers crop their waxen thighs,
                And light them at the fiery glow-worms' eyes,
                To have my love to bed, and to arise;
                And pluck the wings from painted butterflies
                To fan the moonbeams from his sleeping eyes.

Bottom is delighted with his new companions, and greets them boisterously. Titania commands them to silence her mortal consort and lead him out of the damp night air to her leafy shelter.

> *"... it is interesting that the only human being in the play who comes into direct contact with the fairy world is not any member of Theseus' court or one of the lovers, but Bottom the weaver. The incongruity of bringing the grossest element in the human world into contact with the gossamer world of the fairies is exploited by Shakespeare with delicate brilliance."*
>
> David Daiches, *A Critical History of English Literature*, 1960

Puck realises his mistake

Puck returns to tell Oberon the good news: Titania is now in love with a ridiculous creature, half man and half ass. Oberon is delighted. Puck reports that he has also put the potion from the magical flower into the Athenian's eyes, as commanded.

Two mortals now appear. Oberon recognises the man as the cruel Athenian whom he wished to punish; but Puck does not. The two are Demetrius and Hermia. Hermia is desperate to know where Lysander is. She knows that he was devoted to her, and the only possible explanation for his disappearance, she believes, is that Demetrius has murdered him. For his part, Demetrius is uninterested in his rival's fate; he wants Hermia to love him and forget about Lysander.

Hermia rushes off furiously. Demetrius realises that it is hopeless to try to communicate with her in her current state of agitation, and does not follow. Long nights spent worrying about winning Hermia's love have taken their toll: now, finally, he lies down in the wood and sleeps.

Oberon is displeased. By casting his spell on the wrong man, Puck has not only failed to help Helena but has apparently managed to create discord between two different, faithful lovers. He sends Puck off at once to find Helena, and in the meantime ensures, with his love-potion, that the sleeping Demetrius will fall in love with her when she returns:

Oberon: Flower of this purple dye,
　　　　　Hit with Cupid's archery,
　　　　　Sink in apple of his eye.
　　　　　When his love he doth espy,
　　　　　Let her shine as gloriously
　　　　　As the Venus of the sky.
　　　　　When thou wak'st, if she be by,
　　　　　Beg of her for remedy.*

* to ease your heartache, by returning your love

"If Oberon's liquor literally induces characters to perceive each other differently, this after all is exactly what Theseus demands of the rebellious Hermia at the beginning of the play, to see through her father's eyes. The law is, in this sense, quite as fantastical as any fairyland hallucination..."

Terry Eagleton, *William Shakespeare*, 1986

Another admirer for Helena

It only takes Puck a few minutes to search the wood, find Helena and lead her, unwitting, back to Oberon. She is followed by Lysander, who is still ardently declaring his love for her.

Puck is enjoying the confusion, and is eager to see what happens when Demetrius wakes up:

Puck: Shall we their fond* pageant see?
Lord, what fools these mortals be!

* *foolish*

Helena is becoming more and more exasperated at Lysander's insistence. Even if he means what he says, his promises are of no value, considering his betrayal of Hermia:

Helena: Weigh oath with oath, and you will nothing weigh:
Your vows to her and me, put in two scales,
Will even weigh; and both as light as tales.*
Lysander: I had no judgement when to her I swore.
Helena: Nor none, in my mind, now you give her o'er.**

* *rumours, gossip*
** *reject her*

The clamour of their argument wakes Demetrius, and the love-potion in his eyes instantly proves effective:

Demetrius: O Helen, goddess, nymph, perfect, divine!
To what, my love, shall I compare thine eyne?*
Crystal is muddy...

* *eyes*

Helena is distraught. It was bad enough when Lysander pretended to be besotted with her; now it is clear that Demetrius is in on the joke. Clearly, the two of them are aiming to humiliate her for their own amusement. Helena cannot hold back her tears.

The two men now confront one another. Lysander tells Demetrius to leave Helena alone; he is welcome to Hermia, whom he was recently so keen to marry. Demetrius replies that his love for Hermia was nothing more than a brief aberration. Helena, meanwhile, is appalled that the two of them are taking their practical joke to such extremes.

The two friends fall out

Hermia, guided through the night by the sound of Lysander's voice, now arrives to join the others. She is relieved to find Lysander alive and well, but puzzled that he should have left her alone, sleeping, in the dark wood.

Lysander's response is dismissive. He is angry that she has followed him, and her presence irritates him. It is obvious why he has left her, he tells Hermia bluntly; Helena is so beautiful, and his love for her so powerful, that he could not do otherwise.

Hermia refuses to believe what she is hearing. As far as Helena is concerned, though, this apparent dismay is clearly a pretence; Hermia too is part of the conspiracy to make a fool of her.

Considering their lifelong friendship, Helena points out, it is shameful that Hermia should take part in such a malicious trick:

Helena: ... we grew together,
            Like to a double cherry, seeming parted,
            But yet an union in partition,
            Two lovely berries moulded on one stem;
            So, with two seeming bodies, but one heart...
            And will you rent our ancient* love asunder
            To join with men in scorning your poor friend?

            * *enduring, long-standing*

Hermia is bewildered by her friend's accusation, and tries to contradict her. But Helena is by now in full flow. Not only is Hermia part of this conspiracy, she alleges, but it was her idea in the first place to persuade her two admirers to feign love for poor Helena, ugly and unlovable as she is. Hermia's denial only makes Helena more convinced that they are all trying to make fun of her.

Demetrius and Lysander now start arguing, each claiming to be more in love with Helena than the other. Hermia's attempts to question her beloved Lysander are met with contempt and spite. Finally, she realises that Lysander is not joking. Her self-control vanishes, and she turns on Helena in a fit of jealous fury:

Lysander: ... be out of hope, of question, of doubt;
            Be certain, nothing truer; 'tis no jest
            That I do hate thee, and love Helena.
Hermia: O me! [*To Helena.*] You juggler!* You canker-blossom!**
            You thief of love! What, have you come by night
            And stol'n my love's heart from him?

            * *swindler, trickster*
            ** *worm, grub that destroys blossoms*

Still convinced that she is the victim of a malicious joke, Helena snaps back at Hermia. Her comment on Hermia's size touches a raw nerve:

> *Helena:* Fie, fie, you counterfeit! You puppet* you!
> *Hermia:* 'Puppet'! Why, so? Ay, that way goes the game!
> Now I perceive that she hath made compare
> Between our statures; she hath urg'd her height;**
> And with her personage, her tall personage,
> Her height, forsooth, she hath prevail'd with him.
> ... How low am I, thou painted maypole? Speak:
> How low am I? I am not yet so low
> But that my nails can reach unto thine eyes.
>
> * *little doll*
> ** *used her tallness as an argument in her favour*

Alarmed at Hermia's frenzy, Helena calls out for help, and the two men contend to protect her. By now Helena has had enough. She confesses the truth to Hermia, and admits that she revealed Hermia's secret elopement to Demetrius, hoping to gain his gratitude: all she wants now, however, is to be left in peace and allowed to return quietly to Athens. Nevertheless, she cannot resist a final provocative comment as she warns her defenders to be on their guard:

> *Helena:* O, when she is angry, she is keen and shrewd;*
> She was a vixen when she went to school,
> And though she be but little, she is fierce.
> *Hermia:* 'Little' again? Nothing but 'low' and 'little'?
>
> * *aggressive and spiteful*

Demetrius and Lysander, who are becoming increasingly truculent over Helena, now march out to fight a duel. Helena, unwilling to be alone with her irate friend, makes a hasty exit:

Hermia: You, mistress, all this coil is long of you.*
Nay, go not back.**
Helena: I will not trust you, I,
Nor longer stay in your curst company.
Your hands than mine are quicker for a fray:
My legs are longer though, to run away.

* all this turmoil is your fault
** don't back away from me

Hermia follows her, bewildered at the madness that has suddenly swept over them all.

Violence is averted

Oberon and Puck have been observing the antics of the humans. Puck is enjoying the spectacle, but the Fairy King is troubled. To prevent the duel between the rival lovers, he orders his attendant to conjure up a thick fog throughout the wood, and, by imitating their voices, to lead the two men away from one another. He gives Puck a herb which will counteract the love-potion. When Lysander falls asleep, Puck is to pour the herb's juice into the young man's eyes, so that his infatuation with Helena will vanish, and harmony will be restored:

Oberon: When they next wake, all this derision
Shall seem a dream and fruitless vision...

Puck wonders if there is time to do all this before dawn. Oberon reminds him that, as fairies rather than ghosts or evil spirits, they are free to roam after daybreak:

Puck: ... yonder shines Aurora's harbinger,*
At whose approach, ghosts wandering here and there
Troop home to churchyards. Damned spirits all,
That in cross-ways** and floods have burial,
Already to their wormy beds are gone,
For fear lest day should look their shames upon...

Oberon: But we are spirits of another sort:
I with the Morning's love have oft made sport...

* the morning star, heralding the arrival of the dawn
** crossroads

Oberon sets off to acquire the changeling boy from the spellbound Titania. The two rivals for Helena's love now stumble in, unable to find one another in the gloom. Puck challenges and taunts them, imitating each one's voice in turn, and soon has the two of them running round helplessly in circles. Eventually they both give up, exhausted, and lie down to sleep on the ground.

Damned spirits all,
That in cross-ways and floods have burial...

Suicide was considered a mortal sin in Elizabethan times. Those who had taken their own lives could not be given a Christian burial in consecrated ground; traditionally, they were buried at crossroads along public highways. Where suicide was by drowning, the body was often left to decompose in the water.

Shakespeare makes it clear that the fairies, though mischievous and amoral, do not belong to the world of condemned spirits, who were widely believed to wander from their graves under cover of darkness.

Helena wanders in next, weary and miserable, longing for daylight so that she can make her way back to Athens, and escape the torment that her companions have been inflicting on her. She too lies down, unaware of the two men nearby, and falls asleep.

Finally Hermia staggers in, wet and tired, her clothes in tatters after her fruitless chase through the dark wood. She settles down to sleep, with a brief prayer that Lysander will not be hurt if he and Demetrius should fight.

All four young Athenians are now asleep on the ground after their lunatic night in the wood. Puck approaches Lysander and chants a spell as he pours the antidote into his eyes:

> *Puck:*   When thou wak'st,
> Thou tak'st
> True delight
> In the sight
> Of thy former lady's eye;
> And the country proverb known,
> That every man should take his own,
> In your waking shall be shown:
>   Jack shall have Jill,
>   Nought shall go ill...

Bottom in clover IV, i

Bottom, enjoying the devoted attention of Titania and her fairies, is basking in the lap of luxury.

The Queen has decked his ass-head with roses, and is fondly stroking his cheeks and ears. He is keeping his attendants busy with tasks and errands.

> *"Bottom is neither more nor less oblivious in the ass's head; this head is the palpable extension of his native condition... he steers an undeviating course through the ordinary and the marvellous alike."*
>
> Bertrand Evans, *Shakespeare's Comedies*, 1960

One fairy is sent off to fetch some honey:

Bottom: Mounsieur Cobweb, good mounsieur, get you your weapons in your hand, and kill me a red-hipped humble-bee on the top of a thistle; and good mounsieur, bring me the honey-bag... have a care the honey-bag break not; I would be loath to have you overflowen* with a honey-bag, signior.

* engulfed, drowned

Two other fairies are instructed to give him a good scratch around the head:

Bottom: I must to the barber's, mounsieur, for methinks I am marvellous hairy about the face; and I am such a tender ass, if my hair do but tickle me, I must scratch.

Titania affectionately asks her love what he would like to eat. His tastes have changed along with his appearance, and he declares that nothing can beat a bundle of good, sweet hay. However, he is starting to feel drowsy, and Titania orders the fairies away:

Bottom: ... I pray you, let none of your people stir me: I have an exposition of sleep come upon me.

Titania: Sleep thou, and I will wind thee in my arms.
Fairies, be gone, and be all ways away.
So doth the woodbine the sweet honeysuckle
Gently entwist; the female ivy so
Enrings the barky fingers of the elm.
O how I love thee! How I dote on thee!

The King and Queen are reunited

Bottom and Titania settle down to sleep, the Queen clinging tenderly to her new love.

Oberon and Puck come forward to observe the slumbering Queen. Oberon is starting to feel sorry for her, he admits, revealing that he has finally persuaded her to give him the changeling child. He had found her picking fresh young flowers for her beloved; he had scolded her, and she, more interested in pleasing her new sweetheart than in arguing with Oberon, had meekly agreed to his demand for the boy. Oberon now resolves to release Titania from her grotesque devotion, and squeezes juice from the remedial herb into her eyes.

Waking, Titania is relieved to see Oberon, and immediately starts to tell him of the bizarre dream she has just had. It was no dream, says Oberon: he points to the sleeping figure of Bottom, and Titania recoils in disgust.

It is now time to return Nick Bottom the weaver to his old self, decides Oberon, and he tells Puck to remove the man's ass-head. He calls for soft music, to send Bottom and the four lovers into an even deeper sleep.

Once the mortals are completely under its soporific spell, Oberon calls for the music to become louder and livelier, and he and his Queen dance to celebrate their own reconciliation, and the weddings soon to take place in Athens:

Oberon: Come my queen, take hands with me,
And rock the ground whereon these sleepers be.
Now thou and I are new in amity,
And will to-morrow midnight, solemnly,
Dance in Duke Theseus' house triumphantly,
And bless it to all fair prosperity.
There shall the pairs of faithful lovers be
Wedded, with Theseus, all in jollity.

The lark is singing, and the morning is on its way. It is time for the fairies to leave the wood and head westwards, following the night around the globe.

> *"For all the literary mastery of the play, its principal turning-point is the wordless dance that marks the reunion of Oberon and Titania."*
>
> Stanley Wells, *Shakespeare: A Dramatic Life*, 1994

Daylight returns

The blare of hunting-horns sounds through the clear air of the midsummer morning. Theseus and Hippolyta, up early to celebrate the break of day, are out hunting in the Athenian wood.

The air is fresh and invigorating, and the two hunters, enjoying the clamorous barking of the hounds, are in high spirits:

Theseus: We will, fair queen, up to the mountain's top
And mark the musical confusion
Of hounds and echo in conjunction.
Hippolyta: I was with Hercules and Cadmus once,
When in a wood of Crete they bay'd* the bear
With hounds of Sparta; never did I hear
Such gallant chiding; for, besides the groves,
The skies, the fountains, every region near
Seem'd all one mutual cry; I never heard
So musical a discord, such sweet thunder.

* *cornered, held at bay*

Theseus tells Hippolyta proudly that his own hounds are of the same Spartan pedigree. Above all, he loves the harmony of their baying, regardless of their lack of speed:

Theseus: ... their heads are hung
                With ears that sweep away the morning dew...
                Slow in pursuit, but match'd in mouth like bells,
                Each under each:* a cry more tuneable
                Was never holla'd to, nor cheer'd with horn,
                In Crete, in Sparta, nor in Thessaly.

* like a group of bells, each with a different pitch

Theseus notices a group of slumbering figures on the ground. Egeus, escorting the Duke, is startled to discover that one of them is his daughter Hermia: he then recognises the others as her two admirers, Lysander and Demetrius, and her friend Helena.

The Duke assumes that the young people have come into the wood, as he and Hippolyta did, to celebrate the midsummer dawn. Seeing Hermia, he is reminded that she must give her decision today, choosing whether she will obey her father and marry Demetrius, or spend the rest of her life in a nunnery.

Theseus calls for the hunting-horns to be sounded again, and the four sleepers awake. Shocked at finding themselves in the Duke's presence, they kneel at once, but Theseus asks them to stand. He is intrigued that Demetrius and Lysander seem to be friends, knowing that they are rivals for Hermia's love.

Lysander is the first to speak. He is confused, he admits, and cannot immediately remember how he came to be in the wood. Then he recalls that he and Hermia came together, aiming to run away from Athens and the Athenian law.

Egeus interrupts, incensed, calling on the Duke to punish Lysander with the full force of the law for his illicit venture. However, Demetrius, to Egeus' dismay, does not take his side. He reveals that his feelings for Helena have undergone a mysterious, profound change:

Demetrius: ... I in fury hither follow'd them,
                Fair Helena in fancy* following me.
                But my good lord, I wot** not by what power -
                But by some power it is - my love to Hermia,
                Melted as the snow, seems to me now
                As the remembrance of an idle gaud***
                Which in my childhood I did dote upon;
                And all the faith, the virtue of my heart,
                The object and the pleasure of mine eye,
                Is only Helena.

    * *love*
    ** *know*
    *** *toy, trinket*

Theseus realises, with great satisfaction, that the situation has resolved itself. Demetrius no longer wishes to marry Hermia, so she is free to marry Lysander. The Duke overrules Egeus: neither Hermia nor Lysander will be punished. Instead, Theseus proposes that the two couples will be married alongside Hippolyta and himself, in a joint ceremony. He calls off the hunt, and invites all those present to return with him to Athens.

The four lovers, alone in the wood, are still dazed. Unsure of what has really happened and what has been imagined, they suspect at first that they are still dreaming:

Demetrius: These things seem small and undistinguishable,
        Like far-off mountains turned into clouds.
                          ... Are you sure
        That we are awake? It seems to me
        That yet* we sleep, we dream. Do you not think
        The Duke was here, and bid us follow him?
Hermia: Yea, and my father.
Helena: And Hippolyta.
Lysander: And he did bid us follow to the temple.

        * *still*

Between them, they decide that they are now awake and in the real world. They set off to follow the Duke.

> *"In the violent contrast between the erotic madness liberated by the night and the censorship of day which orders everything to be forgotten, Shakespeare seems most ahead of his time."*
>
> Jan Kott, *Shakespeare Our Contemporary*, 1965

Bottom's Dream

Bottom awakes with a start. He has not forgotten his cue, he assures everyone, and is ready to come on as soon as Thisbe calls for him. Looking around, he realises that the rehearsal is over: Peter Quince, Flute and the rest have disappeared, leaving him alone in the wood. Then the memories of the night gone by start flooding back:

> *Bottom:* I have had a most rare vision. I have had a dream, past the wit of man to say what dream it was. Man is but an ass if he go about to expound this dream. Methought I was - there is no man can tell what.

He finds it a struggle to piece together the rapidly disappearing details of his dream, but Bottom is convinced that it will make an impressive story. With growing excitement, he develops a grandiose plan for its performance:

> *Bottom:* I will get Peter Quince to write a ballad of this dream: it shall be called 'Bottom's Dream', because it hath no bottom;* and I will sing it in the latter end of a play, before the Duke.
>
> * *it is unfathomable and profound*

"*A dream is the heart of the dreamer's private universe, and is therefore incommunicable. Yet the dreaming power is closely connected with the creative faculties, which are powers of communication. This is the paradox that Bottom struggles with...*"

Northrop Frye, *A Natural Perspective*, 1965

The company is reunited

Back in Athens, Bottom's companions are in a despondent mood. There is no sign of Bottom at his house; the spirits that turned him into an ass have clearly stolen him away. On top of the loss of their friend, the workmen are faced with the inevitable cancellation of their play. No-one else in Athens, they all agree, can carry off the part of Pyramus like Nick Bottom.

Snug the joiner arrives, announcing forlornly that the wedding will be an even bigger occasion than planned, with other couples joining the Duke and Hippolyta in the marriage ceremony. If only Bottom were present, and their play could go ahead, says Snug mournfully, their fortunes would be assured. Flute agrees: once the Duke had seen Bottom's Pyramus, he would undoubtedly have rewarded him with a generous income for life.

The workmen's sad musings are interrupted as Bottom himself bursts in, boisterous as ever.

He greets his overjoyed friends, and is immediately torn between his urge to recount the fantastic events of the night and his rapidly fading memory:

Quince: Bottom! O most courageous day! O most happy hour!
Bottom: Masters, I am to discourse wonders: but ask me not what; for if I tell you, I am not true Athenian. I will tell you everything, right as it fell out.
Quince: Let us hear, sweet Bottom.
Bottom: Not a word of me.

However, Bottom has some exciting news. He has heard that their play is being considered for performance at the Duke's wedding. In fact, as far as he is concerned, it is certain to be requested. He urges his comrades to prepare thoroughly for the big event:

Bottom: ... let Thisbe have clean linen; and let not him that plays the lion pare his nails, for they shall hang out for the lion's claws. And most dear actors, eat no onions nor garlic, for we are to utter sweet breath; and I do not doubt but to hear them say, it is a sweet comedy. No more words. Away!

Like many of Shakespeare's plays, *A Midsummer Night's Dream* was performed in adapted, abridged and rewritten versions for over two hundred years following the author's death. It was not until the 1820s that Shakespeare's original text was used once more for performances.

The play was very popular in Victorian times. Lavish productions with spectacular scenery were then the rule; this trend reached its peak in a 1900 production which featured crowds of children, live rabbits and birds in a sumptuous setting with real bluebells, moss and foliage, illuminated by countless twinkling lights.

One of the many musicians attracted to *A Midsummer Night's Dream* was Felix Mendelssohn, who wrote an overture and incidental music in 1827, at the age of eighteen, for a German production of the play. Like much of Mendelssohn's work, this music soon became popular in Victorian Britain. At the wedding of Queen Victoria's daughter in 1858, Mendelssohn's 'Wedding March', originally written to accompany the entrance of the newly-wed Theseus and Hippolyta, was played as the bride arrived. The fashion quickly spread; the piece written for *A Midsummer Night's Dream* soon became a familiar feature of weddings the length and breadth of the country, and has remained so ever since.

Imagination or reality?

The Duke's wedding-day has arrived. He and Hippolyta are now man and wife, as are Lysander and Hermia, and Demetrius and Helena. The marriage-feast is over, and it will soon be time for the evening's entertainments.

Theseus and Hippolyta are discussing the two young couples' descriptions of their mystifying experiences in the wood. The Duke is sceptical:

> *Hippolyta:* 'Tis strange, my Theseus, that these lovers speak of.
> *Theseus:* More strange than true. I never may believe
> These antique* fables, nor these fairy toys.**
>
> ** archaic, absurd*
> *** stories, tales*

Love, like madness, can produce an endless variety of strange imaginings, believes the Duke. Warming to his theme, he suggests that there are three types of individual whose minds are liable to produce visions of things not present in the real world:

> *Theseus:* The lunatic, the lover, and the poet
> Are of imagination all compact:*
> One sees more devils than vast hell can hold;
> That is the madman: the lover, all as frantic,
> Sees Helen's beauty in a brow of Egypt:**
> The poet's eye, in a fine frenzy rolling,
> Doth glance from heaven to earth, from earth to heaven;
> And as imagination bodies forth
> The forms of things unknown,*** the poet's pen
> Turns them to shapes, and gives to airy nothing
> A local habitation and a name.
>
> ** formed, made up*
> *** sees the beauty of Helen of Troy in a Gipsy's face*
> **** as the poet's imagination gives substance and form*
> *to things that previously existed only as ideas*

Theseus' bride, however, is not convinced that the lovers' stories are entirely imaginary:

> *Hippolyta:* But all the story of the night told over,
> And all their minds transfigur'd so together,*
> More witnesseth than fancy's images,**
> And grows to something of great constancy...***
>
> * *the fact that they all shared in the derangement*
> ** *suggests something more real than delusions created by love*
> *** *their story begins to seem consistent and genuine*

The discussion is interrupted by the arrival of the two young couples.

The lunatic, the lover, and the poet...

Many critics are uneasy at Theseus' rather dismissive attitude towards poetry. Does Shakespeare share the views of his wise, rational Duke?

"... I can see only two redeeming points about Theseus' opinion: that, being himself a lover, he comes under the aim of his own attack, and that this attack upon poetry is conducted, elegantly enough, in poetry."

Howard Nemerov, *The Marriage of Theseus and Hippolyta*, 1956

The Duke makes his choice of entertainment

Theseus is keen to have a play performed, or some music or dancing, to enliven the last few hours of the day. He calls for Philostrate, his Master of the Revels, and asks him what he has planned. Philostrate presents him with a list of the available entertainments. At first, there is nothing that appeals to the Duke:

Theseus: [*Reads.*] 'The battle with the Centaurs, to be sung
By an Athenian eunuch to the harp'?

He decides against this: he was at the battle himself, with his cousin Hercules, and has told his bride the story of the punishment of the drunken, violent Centaurs who had disrupted a wedding-feast. He considers the next item on the list:

Theseus: [*Reads.*] 'The riot of the tipsy Bacchanals,*
Tearing the Thracian singer in their rage'?

* priestesses of Bacchus, god of wine and revelry

This too he dismisses out of hand; the story of the priestesses who tear the legendary poet Orpheus limb from limb in an orgiastic frenzy is an old one, and he has seen it staged before.

Theseus continues, but finds the next item in the list equally unappealing, for different reasons:

Theseus: [*Reads.*] 'The thrice three Muses mourning for the death
          Of Learning, late deceas'd in beggary'?
          That is some satire, keen and critical,
          Not sorting with* a nuptial ceremony.

          * *suitable for, befitting*

The Duke rejects the scathing satire as inappropriate for their wedding celebrations. However, the next item catches his eye:

Theseus: [*Reads.*] 'A tedious brief scene of young Pyramus
          And his love Thisbe, very tragical mirth'?

Theseus is intrigued and amused by the incongruous description. His Master of the Revels, who has seen a run-through of the play, gives his own judgement:

Theseus: Merry and tragical? Tedious and brief?
             That is hot ice, and wondrous strange snow!
             How shall we find the concord of this discord?
Philostrate: A play there is, my lord, some ten words long,
             Which is as brief as I have known a play;
             But by ten words, my lord, it is too long,
             Which makes it tedious; for in all the play
             There is not one word apt, one player fitted.*
             And tragical, my noble lord, it is,
             For Pyramus therein doth kill himself;
             Which, when I saw rehears'd, I must confess
             Made mine eyes water...

             * *suited to his part*

That is some satire, keen and critical...

In 1592, the playwright Robert Greene was dying, at the age of thirty-four, impoverished, homeless, bitter and regretful after a brief, dissolute life. Shortly before his death, he wrote an angry pamphlet addressed to some of his fellow playwrights, university scholars like himself. In it, he denounces various rival playwrights and, in particular, the actors who had made so much money from his plays - or so he claimed - but had done nothing to help him when he fell on hard times.

Greene singles out one actor in particular who, despite his provincial roots and his lack of a university education, has turned successfully to playwriting:

... trust them* not: for there is an upstart Crow, beautified with our feathers, that... supposes he is as well able to bombast out a blank verse as the best of you...

* actors

As Greene's diatribe goes on, it becomes clear that the 'upstart crow' is none other than the twenty-eight year old William Shakespeare, already a major figure in the London theatre.

It is not known how Shakespeare reacted to Greene's vitriolic attack, but he was probably sufficiently confident in his own ability to shrug off the insult. Might Theseus' rejection of the angry tirade which laments 'the death of Learning, late deceas'd in beggary' be Shakespeare's way of giving a gentle but firm rebuff to Greene's scathing outburst?

Theseus is undeterred, and Philostrate's attempts to dissuade him only make him more determined to see the workmen's efforts. He sends his Master of the Revels off to bring in the actors.

Hippolyta is uneasy; she does not want to see the men make fools of themselves. Her husband reassures her that no-one will look foolish if the performance, however poor, is taken in the right spirit. The effort and the sense of duty of the participants are what matters, he believes. There have been times when, on his state visits, those giving him a speech of welcome have floundered, overcome with anxiety, and have been unable to continue. On such occasions he has not taken offence, but has charitably accepted the speaker's good intentions:

> *Theseus:* Where I have come, great clerks have purposed
> To greet me with premeditated welcomes;
> Where I have seen them shiver and look pale,
> Make periods in the midst of sentences,
> Throttle their practis'd accent in their fears,
> And, in conclusion, dumbly have broke off,
> Not paying me a welcome. Trust me, sweet,
> Out of this silence yet I pick'd a welcome...

A fanfare of trumpets announces the arrival on stage of Peter Quince, who is to speak the prologue of the tragedy.

Quince sets the scene

Either through the anxiety that the Duke has just described
or out of sheer incompetence, Quince becomes thoroughly
confused in the delivery of his prologue. Although he
remembers the words correctly, his misuse of punctuation
overturns the sense of his introductory speech, to the
amusement of his audience:

Prologue: ... Our true intent is. All for your delight,
We are not here. That you should here repent you,
The actors are at hand...
Theseus: This fellow doth not stand upon points.*

** does not bother about trivial details; does not take
much notice of punctuation*

The prologue goes on, in traditional style, to introduce the
characters and summarise the plot. Nick Bottom is brought
on as Pyramus, Flute as his lover Thisbe, Snout, covered in
lumps of plaster, as the Wall, Starveling and his lantern as
Moonshine, and Snug as the Lion.

The plot is very simple. Thisbe, on her way to a clandestine
meeting with Pyramus, is frightened by a lion: running off,
she drops her cloak, which the lion tears to shreds. Finding
the tattered cloak, Pyramus, assuming that his lover has
been killed, commits suicide: Thisbe returns and, finding
Pyramus dead, kills herself too. Quince fills out the bare
facts with plenty of lurid, high-flown verse:

Prologue: Anon comes Pyramus, sweet youth and tall,
And finds his trusty Thisbe's mantle slain;
Whereat with blade, with bloody blameful blade,
He bravely broach'd his boiling bloody breast...

The lovers arrange a secret meeting

The prologue over, Peter Quince and the company leave the stage, and the play begins. First on is Wall, who introduces himself at some length:

Wall: In this same interlude* it doth befall
That I, one Snout by name, present a wall;
And such a wall as I would have you think
That had in it a crannied hole, or chink,
Through which the lovers, Pyramus and Thisbe,
Did whisper often, very secretly.

* play

Pyramus comes on next, addressing first the night and then the wall. He asks the wall to show his chink so that he can look for his beloved Thisbe on the other side. Snout obligingly stretches out his fingers, and Pyramus peers through.

Unable to see his love, Pyramus curses the wall angrily. Theseus suggests that the wall, which evidently has feelings of its own, should curse back at him. Overhearing his comment, Bottom steps out of character and politely corrects the Duke; it is Thisbe's turn to speak next, not Wall's. Thisbe does indeed enter, on cue, and she and Pyramus affirm their undying love. Unable to reach each other through the wall, and forbidden from coming together by the hostility of their parents, they plan without further ado to meet secretly, away from the city, at Ninus' tomb:

Pyramus: O kiss me through the hole of this vile wall.
Thisbe: I kiss the wall's hole, not your lips at all.
Pyramus: Wilt thou at Ninny's tomb meet me straightway?
Thisbe: 'Tide life, 'tide death,* I come without delay.

* come life or death

Wall, his part in the play now over, makes a dignified exit. Theseus remarks that the wall between the warring families is now demolished; Demetrius suggests that it deserved its fate for failing to pass on news of the lovers' escape to their parents.

By now, Hippolyta is finding the amateurishness of the production unbearable. Her husband replies that it is all a matter of perception:

> *Hippolyta:* This is the silliest stuff that ever I heard.
> *Theseus:* The best in this kind* are but shadows; and the worst are no worse, if imagination amend them.
> *Hippolyta:* It must be your imagination then, and not theirs.
> *Theseus:* If we imagine no worse of them than they of themselves, they may pass for excellent men.
>
> * *even the best actors*

Two new characters make their way on stage, and the Duke and his wife discontinue their debate.

The tragedy of *Pyramus and Thisbe*, as staged by Quince and his troupe of amateur actors, is a story of love, parental opposition, secret meetings, misunderstanding and suicide. It reads suspiciously like a parody of *Romeo and Juliet*, Shakespeare's spectacularly successful tragedy which was first performed, in all probability, earlier the same year.

In depicting the lamentable efforts of Quince, Bottom and the rest, was Shakespeare enjoying a joke at his own expense?

Pyramus and Thisbe meet a tragic end

The Lion and Moonshine enter. Snug reassures the ladies that there is nothing to be afraid of:

Lion: You ladies, you whose gentle hearts do fear
The smallest monstrous mouse that creeps on floor,
May now, perchance, both quake and tremble here,
When lion rough in wildest rage doth roar.
Then know that I as Snug the joiner am
A lion fell...*

** I am Snug the joiner playing the part of a
fearsome lion*

When the celebrations marking the baptism of Prince Henry of Scotland in 1594 were being prepared, a plan to include a chariot drawn by a tame lion was proposed. Fearing that the beast might cause alarm, and possibly run out of control in the ensuing panic, the organisers eventually dropped the scheme.

Shakespeare undoubtedly heard about the episode, and takes the idea one stage further; the presenters of *Pyramus and Thisbe* are even more cautious, fearful of the pandemonium that their illusory lion may cause.

"Quince and his actors quite misconceive the relationship between dramatic illusion, realism, and the imagination of the audience. With their swords and lion, they are afraid of producing an effect which will be mistaken for reality, and so they take measures to destroy the dramatic illusion - the little illusion they were likely to achieve... They do not credit the audience with the power either to imagine, or to discriminate between the imaginary and the real."

Harold F. Brooks, Introduction to the Arden
edition of *A Midsummer Night's Dream*, 1979

It is now the turn of the emaciated Robin Starveling, with his lantern, dog and bundle of sticks, to announce his presence as Moonshine. However, comments from the increasingly restless audience put him off his stride, and he sulkily abandons his script:

Moonshine: This lantern doth the horned* moon present;
Myself the Man i'th'Moon do seem to be...
Hippolyta: I am aweary of this moon. Would he would change!
Theseus: It appears by his small light of discretion** that he is in the wane; but yet in courtesy, in all reason, we must stay the time.***
Lysander: Proceed, Moon.
Moonshine: All that I have to say is, to tell you that the lantern is the moon; I the Man i'th'Moon; this thorn-bush my thorn-bush; and this dog my dog.

* crescent
** by his lack of judgement
*** wait for him to finish; allow the Moon time
to disappear

Thisbe now comes on stage, looking for her beloved Pyramus. Confronted by the roaring Lion, she runs away, and the Lion gnaws at her discarded cloak. The audience cheers them all on, including the disgruntled Starveling:

Demetrius: Well roared, Lion!
Theseus: Well run, Thisbe!
Hippolyta: Well shone, Moon! Truly, the moon shines with a good grace.

The Lion runs off, and Pyramus enters, looking eagerly for his sweetheart. Finding only her bloodstained cloak, he is overcome with woe.

> *"... in the force of his passion, Pyramus leaps to a false conclusion and both lovers commit impulsive suicide. This hilarious short play reminds us of a dark truth: under different circumstances the Athenian lovers, who were also escaping a forbidding father by running into the woods, might also have perished."*
>
> Mary Ellen Lamb, *The Myth of Theseus and the Minotaur*, 1979

As Pyramus rants wildly, Theseus remarks laconically that the speech is almost poignant. His wife, on the other hand, is genuinely moved despite herself:

Pyramus: What dreadful dole is here?
Eyes, do you see?
How can it be?
O dainty duck! O dear!
Thy mantle good,
What! Stain'd with blood?
Approach, ye Furies fell!
O Fates, come, come...

Theseus: This passion, and the death of a dear friend, would go near to make a man look sad.

Hippolyta: Beshrew my heart, but I pity the man.

Bottom now calls on all his dramatic powers as Pyramus kills himself in his anguish:

Pyramus: Come tears, confound!
Out sword, and wound
The pap of Pyramus;
Ay, that left pap,
Where heart doth hop: [*Stabs himself.*]
Thus die I, thus, thus, thus!
Now am I dead...

Finally, several lines later, Pyramus dies. Thisbe returns to find him dead, and, after grieving over his corpse, takes up his sword and stabs herself. The play is over.

The only characters left to bury the dead, Theseus and Demetrius observe, are Moonshine, Lion and the Wall. Bottom, overhearing, cannot resist correcting them, and the dead Pyramus comes suddenly to life to inform the audience that the wall that divided Pyramus and Thisbe is in reality no longer standing, having been destroyed by their grieving parents long ago.

Bottom asks the Duke whether he wishes to hear the play's epilogue or whether they should go straight on to the Bergomask, a comic country dance routine that they have prepared as a finale. Theseus is happy to give the epilogue a miss. The dancing ensues, and the workmen take a final bow before leaving.

The evening draws to an end

The hilarity of the tragedy they have just witnessed has made the evening pass swiftly for the three newly-married couples. It is time for bed, says Theseus:

Theseus: The iron tongue of midnight hath told twelve.
Lovers, to bed; 'tis almost fairy time.*
I fear we shall outsleep the coming morn
As much as we this night have overwatch'd.**
          ... Sweet friends, to bed.
A fortnight hold we this solemnity***
In nightly revels and new jollity.

* the small hours
** stayed awake later than usual
*** celebration

The state rooms of the Duke's palace are left deserted as Theseus and Hippolyta, the young couples, and the lords, courtiers and attendants all make their way to bed.

Spirits inhabit the palace

It is indeed fairy time, as Theseus said: and Puck now arrives in the darkness of the palace. He describes the eerie night-time world inhabited by the fairies:

Puck: Now the hungry lion roars,
And the wolf behowls the moon;
Whilst the heavy ploughman snores,
All with weary task fordone.*
... Now it is the time of night
That the graves, all gaping wide,
Every one lets forth his sprite
In the church-way paths to glide.
And we fairies, that do run
By the triple Hecate's team**
From the presence of the sun,
Following darkness like a dream,
Now are frolic...***

exhausted
** *alongside the team of dragons that draw the chariot of Hecate, goddess of night, who takes different forms in her three realms of the sky, the land and the underworld*
*** *free to play*

Although he is a mischievous spirit by nature, he has come tonight to carry out one of his traditional good turns, the secret sweeping away of dust from the house.

The Fairy King and Queen now arrive in the Duke's palace, followed by their attendants. Titania instructs the fairies to join hands, and the King and Queen lead as they sing and dance in celebration of the day's weddings.

The dancing over, Oberon directs the fairies to run nimbly through the palace, by the pale, glimmering light of their torches, and bestow blessings on all the sleeping inhabitants. He proclaims that the newly-married couples will be true to one another, and their children free from disfigurement and ominous birthmarks:

Titania: ... Hand in hand, with fairy grace,
              Will we sing, and bless this place.
Oberon: Now, until the break of day,
              Through this house each fairy stray.
              To the best bride-bed* will we,
              Which by us shall blessed be...
              So shall all the couples three
              Ever true in loving be;
              And the blots of Nature's hand
              Shall not in their issue** stand...

              * the bed of Theseus and Hippolyta
              ** shall not harm their offspring

Finally, Oberon gives the fairies dew from the fields to sprinkle, in blessing, throughout the palace. He tells them all to gather again at daybreak, when they will depart into the night once more, returning the palace to its mortal inhabitants.

"Not all fires to be seen on Midsummer Eve were illusory. The man-made fires were called 'blessing fires'. Leaping through them or dancing round them was supposed to ensure fertility, innocence, good luck, and easy childbirth. Torches kindled at these fires were carried in processions and used to light hearth-fires. These associations are gathered in at the end of A Midsummer Night's Dream *when the fairies re-enter to bless the marriage... However, Shakespeare here performs a reversal. Such blessings were usually intended to keep fairies and other spirits away, since it was thought that they might interfere in matters of fertility and childbearing, perhaps even steal children for their own use. That the fairies perform the purification themselves emphasises their ultimate benevolence."*

David Young, *Something of Great Constancy*, 1966

Puck has the last word

The spirits set off, leaving Puck alone on the stage to address the audience. If the subject matter of the play has displeased us, he says, there is a simple remedy:

Puck: If we shadows* have offended,
        Think but this, and all is mended,
        That you have but slumber'd here
        While these visions did appear.

spirits, fairies; actors

If we choose, we can believe, like Nick Bottom, that the whole thing has been no more than a puzzling dream. Perhaps, like Duke Theseus - in whose very palace Puck is now standing - we do not even believe in the fairy world. In any case, Puck asks for our good will:

Puck: Give me your hands, if we be friends,
        And Robin shall restore amends.*

Robin Goodfellow - Puck - will treat us kindly

If we applaud, promises Puck, on his word of honour, we will never again be troubled by the mischievous fairies.

Acknowledgements

The following publications have proved invaluable as sources of factual information and critical insight:

- Charles Boyce, *Shakespeare A to Z*, Roundtable Press, 1990

- Harold F. Brooks, Introduction to the Arden Shakespeare edition of *A Midsummer Night's Dream*, Methuen, 1979

- David Daiches, *A Critical History of English Literature*, Secker and Warburg, 1960

- Terry Eagleton, *William Shakespeare*, Blackwell, 1986

- Bertrand Evans, *Shakespeare's Comedies*, Oxford University Press, 1960

- Levi Fox, *The Shakespeare Handbook*, Mobius International, 1987

- Northrop Frye, *A Natural Perspective: The Development of Shakespearean Comedy and Romance*, Columbia University Press, 1965

- Harley Granville-Barker, Preface to the Players' Shakespeare edition of *A Midsummer Night's Dream*, Ernest Benn, 1924

- Jan Kott, *Shakespeare Our Contemporary*, Doubleday, 1965

- Mary Ellen Lamb, *A Midsummer Night's Dream: The Myth of Theseus and the Minotaur*, Texas Studies in Literature and Language, 1979

- Howard Nemerov, *The Marriage of Theseus and Hippolyta*, Yale University Press, 1956

- Mark W. Scott and Laurie Lanzen Harris, *Shakespearean Criticism*, Gale Research, 1986

- Caroline Spurgeon, *Shakespeare's Imagery and What It Tells Us*, Cambridge University Press, 1935

- Peter Thomson, *Shakespeare's Professional Career*, Cambridge University Press, 1992

- Stanley Wells, Introduction to the New Penguin Shakespeare edition of *A Midsummer Night's Dream*, Penguin, 1967

- Stanley Wells, *Shakespeare: A Dramatic Life*, Sinclair-Stevenson, 1994

- John Dover Wilson, *Life in Shakespeare's England*, Cambridge University Press, 1911

- David Young, *Something of Great Constancy: The Art of* A Midsummer Night's Dream, Oxford University Press, 1966

All quotations from *A Midsummer Night's Dream* are taken from the Arden Shakespeare.

You can order the *Shakespeare Handbooks*, post free, direct from the publisher. Simply send details of the books you require, together with a cheque or postal order for the total cost, to:

Upstart Crow Publications
11, St John's Terrace
Lewes, East Sussex
BN7 2DL

Phone / fax: 01273 477626

Free postage & packing in the UK.
Overseas customers please allow £1 per book.

———————————

Titles currently available in the *Shakespeare Handbooks* series are:

☐ **Antony & Cleopatra** (ISBN 1 899747 02 8, £3.99)

☐ **As You Like It** (ISBN 1 899747 00 1, £3.99)

☐ **Hamlet** (ISBN 1 899747 07 9, £3.99)

☐ **King Lear** (ISBN 1 899747 03 6, £3.99)

☐ **Macbeth** (ISBN 1 899747 04 4, £3.99)

☐ **A Midsummer Night's Dream** (ISBN 1 899747 09 5, £3.99)

☐ **Romeo & Juliet** (ISBN 1 899747 10 9, £3.99)

☐ **Twelfth Night** (ISBN 1 899747 01 X, £3.99)

———————————

Please make cheques / postal orders payable to **Upstart Crow Publications**.

Upstart Crow Publications will not pass your address on to other organisations.

Prices correct at time of going to press. Whilst every effort is made to keep prices low, Upstart Crow Publications reserves the right to show new retail prices on covers which may differ from those previously advertised in the text or elsewhere.